Makoçe Wiçaŋhpi Wowapi

D(L)akota Star Map
Constellation Guidebook

An Introduction to D(L)akota Star Knowledge

Annette S. Lee
Jim Rock
Charlene O'Rourke

Makoče Wičaŋȟpi Wowapi – D(L)akota Star Map Constellation Guidebook

First published in June 2014
Layout and editing by A. M. Fellegy, Avenue F Productions, Cloquet MN 55720
The LakotaLSU font used to print this work is available from Linguist's
Software, Inc., PO Box 580, Edmonds, WA 98020-0580 USA. Telephone (425)
775-1130, www.linguistsoftware.com.
Printed by Lightning Source-Ingram Spark, North Rocks, CA 99999

Cover art: *Makoče Wičaŋȟpi Wowapi – D(L)akota Star Map* by Annette S. Lee
and Jim Rock

ISBN 978-0-692-23254-5

http://web.stcloudstate.edu/planetarium/native_skywatchers.html

Makoçe Wiçaŋhpi Wowapi

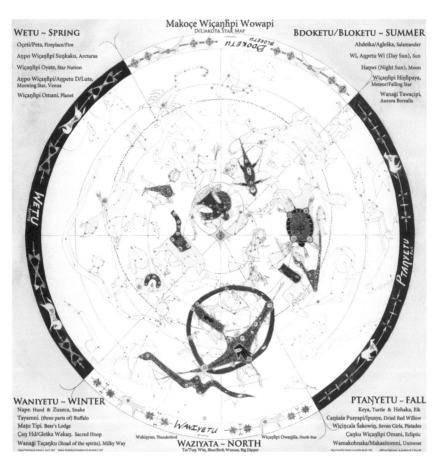

WETU ~ SPRING

Oçeti/Peta, Fireplace/Fire

Aŋpo Wiçaŋĥpi Suŋkaku, Arcturus

Wiçaŋĥpi Oyate, Star Nation

Aŋpo Wiçaŋĥpi/Aŋpetu D/Luta, Morning Star, Venus

Wiçaŋĥpi Omani, Planet

Makoçe Wiçaŋĥpi Wowapi
D(L)AKOTA STAR MAP

BDOKETU/BLOKETU ~ SUMMER

Ahdeśka/Agleśka, Salamander

Wi, Aŋpetu Wi (Day Sun), Sun

Haŋwi (Night Sun), Moon

Wiçaŋĥpi Hiŋĥpaya, Meteor/Falling Star

Wanaǧi Tawaçipi, Aurora Borealis

WANIYETU ~ WINTER

Nape, Hand & Zuzeca, Snake

Tayamni. (three parts of) Buffalo

Maṭo Tipi, Bear's Lodge

Çaŋ Hd/Gleśka Wakaŋ, Sacred Hoop

Wanaǧi Taçaŋku (Road of the spirits), Milky Way

Wakiŋyan, Thunderbird

WAZIYATA ~ NORTH
Tu/Tuŋ Wiŋ, Blue/Birth Woman, Big Dipper

Wiçaŋĥpi Owaŋjila, North Star

PTAŊYETU ~ FALL

Keya, Turtle & Hehaka, Elk

Caŋiaśa Pusyapi/Iṗusye, Dried Red Willow

Wiçiŋçala Śakowiŋ, Seven Girls, Pleiades

Çaŋku Wiçaŋĥpi Omani, Ecliptic

Wamakohnaka/Makasitomni, Universe

Fig. 1. Makoçe Wiçaŋĥpi Wowapi - D(L)akota Star Map

INTRODUCTION

Native Skywatchers

In the Ojibwe language, the Big Dipper is known as *Ojiig,* the Fisher [1], and in D(L)akota star knowledge, the same group of stars is seen as *To Wiŋ/Tuŋ Wiŋ,* Blue Woman/Birth Woman [2]. In each, there are stories and teachings that help guide, teach, and inspire native peoples. This book is an outgrowth of Native Skywatchers research and programming, which focuses on understanding the Ojibwe and D(L)akota importance of these and other celestial connections. We seek to address the crisis of the loss of the indigenous star knowledge, specifically the Dakota and Ojibwe who are the native peoples of Minnesota. Our purpose is to remember, rebuild, and revitalize the native star knowledge.

There is urgency to this project for two reasons: 1) Native star knowledge is disappearing as elders pass. One Ojibwe elder spoke of his vision of "the star medicine returning through the native youth." He specifically called them "star readers" [3]. In 2011, he passed away suddenly. 2) The Minnesota State Science Standards for K-12 education require an "understanding that men and women throughout the history of all cultures, including Minnesota American Indian tribes and communities, have been involved in engineering design and scientific inquiry. . . .for example, Ojibwe and Dakota knowledge and use of patterns in the stars to predict and plan" [4]; yet, there is a complete lack of materials.

As with many North American tribes, much cultural knowledge, especially cultural astronomy, has been lost. The goal of the Native Skywatchers programming is to build community around native star knowledge. Native Skywatchers research and programming seeks out and brings together elders, culture teachers, language experts, and community members to discuss Ojibwe and D(L)akota star knowledge. Together, we have created two astronomically accurate and culturally important star maps, *Ojibwe Giizhig Anung Masinaa' igan* – Ojibwe Sky Star Map and *Makoçe Wiçaŋhpi Wowapi* – D(L)akota Star Map, which were first disseminated to regional educators at a Native Skywatchers Middle School Teacher workshop in June 2012. In addition, we have developed hands-on curriculum that combines astronomy, culture, language, and art.

1

Sacred Star Sites

STAR/SKY/SPIRIT WORLD

ABOVE

BELOW

EARTH/MATERIAL WORLD

Fig. 2. Diagram of Kapemni

Much of D(L)akota star knowledge rests on the framework of mirroring; it is said, "As it is above (in the sky), it is below (on the Earth)." *Kapemni* can mean swinging around, twisting, or mirroring in D(L)akota [5] and is illustrated by two tipis/triangles connected at their apexes. The inverted top tipi symbolizes the sky/star world. The lower tipi symbolizes the Earth/physical world that we see around us. At the apex where the two worlds/tipis meet is a doorway. When D(L)akota people on Earth mirror what is happening in the stars, a spiritual doorway opens up because of this connection. It is understood that the healing power of the star nation, "the *woniya of Wakaŋ Taŋka,*" flows through [6].

There are many specific sacred sites found in the Dakotas and Minnesota that are the *kapemni* pairs of particular constellations. For example, *Pte He Ġi,* Grey Horn Butte/Grey Buffalo Horn (Devil's Tower) in Wyoming, is the sacred star site that is the *kapemni* pair of *Maṭo Tipila* – Bear's Lodge (Gemini) constellation.

Fig. 3. Pte He Ġi, Grey Horn Butte/Grey Buffalo Horn

Another sacred site is a cave, found in St. Paul, Minnesota and known as *Wakaŋ Tipi,* along the Mississippi River. Jim Rock's Sisseton Dakota father and other Dakota relatives and elders, such as Gary Cavendar, were taught, believed, and said, "We Dakotas come from a cave or a star in Orion's belt or we have always been here." Rock believes these three ideas are simultaneously true because the cave by the river mirrors the star by the Milky Way. Because of this Sky-Earth mirror principle, the *Wakaŋ Tipi* cave by the Big Waterfalls

Fig. 4. Wakaŋ Tipi cave, St. Paul, MN

River *(Haha Wakpa/Wakpa Taŋka/Misi Zibi)* mirrors the Orion's belt origin star (in the *Tayamni* constellation) by the Milky Way Road of Spirits. For Rock, the tipi poles lean together to connect and point us from specific places where the rivers join on Earth Mother below to Sky Father above, so we always live together as good relatives. Rock also believes that the three tipi poles represent not only the three stars in *Tayamni* (as Elmer Running stated), but may also be a tripod of symbolic truths where the River is the Milky Way in the star-filled and sacred cottonwood tree.

Fig. 5. Cottonwood tree in winter

Fig. 6. Cottonwood leaves in summer

Fig. 7. Cross sections of the cottonwood, "Star Tree"

About the D(L)akota Star Map

The D(L)akota map, *Makoçe Wiçaŋhpi Wowapi* – D(L)akota Star Map was created by Annette S. Lee and Jim Rock. The map is primarily based on the chart found in the book *Lakota Star Knowledge* by R. Goodman and his interviews with many Lakota elders [7].

Makoçe Wiçaŋhpi Wowapi – D(L)akota Star Map is organized with Polaris, the North Star, in the center. This emphasizes the closeness of Polaris to our current North Celestial Pole and circumpolar motion. Because of circumpolar motion, we appear to see all the stars in the night sky revolve around the North Star in a counterclockwise motion as the hours pass each night into day. Because of this motion, in some native cultures the North Star is seen as one of the leaders of the star nation. Stars near the North Star do not set below the horizon. These are referred to as "North Circumpolar Stars." Note that the "northern stars" referred to in this book are the circumpolar stars as seen from approximately 45-55° N latitude, 85-110° W longitudes.

All stars not circumpolar, as seen from 45-55° N latitude, rise in the East and set in the West at regular times throughout the year. They are seasonal stars. The

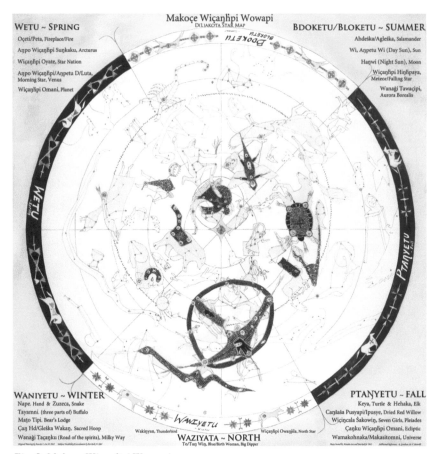

WETU ~ SPRING

Oçeti/Peta, Fireplace/Fire

Aŋpo Wiçaŋhpi Suŋkaku, Arcturus

Wiçaŋhpi Oyate, Star Nation

Aŋpo Wiçaŋhpi/Aŋpetu D/Luta, Morning Star, Venus

Wiçaŋhpi Omani, Planet

Makoçe Wiçaŋhpi Wowapi
D(L)AKOTA STAR MAP

BDOKETU/BLOKETU ~ SUMMER

Ahdeška/Agleška, Salamander

Wi, Aŋpetu Wi (Day Sun), Sun

Haŋwi (Night Sun), Moon

Wiçaŋhpi Hiŋhipaya, Meteor/Falling Star

Wanaǧi Tawaçipi, Aurora Borealis

WANIYETU ~ WINTER

Nape, Hand & Zuzeca, Snake

Tayamni, (three parts of) Buffalo

Maṭo Tipi, Bear's Lodge

Çaŋ Hd/Gleška Wakaŋ, Sacred Hoop

Wanaǧi Taçaŋku (Road of the spirits), Milky Way

WAZIYATA ~ NORTH
To/Tuŋ Wiŋ, Blue/Birth Woman, Big Dipper

Wakiŋyan, Thunderbird

Wiçaŋhpi Owaŋjila, North Star

PTAŊYETU ~ FALL

Keya, Turtle & Hehaka, Elk

Caŋšaša Pusyapi/Ipusye, Dried Red Willow

Wiçiŋcala Šakowiŋ, Seven Girls, Pleiades

Çaŋku Wiçaŋhpi Omani, Ecliptic

Wamakohnaka/Makasitomni, Universe

Fig. 8. *Makoçe Wiçaŋhpi Wowapi*

Makoçe Wiçaŋhpi Wowapi – D(L)akota Star Map is arranged in order to show the constellations that are best visible each season. This assumes a viewing time of a few hours after sunset. In the night sky, stars of each season can be seen best overhead or in the South during that particular season. For example, if you look at the stars in the early summertime a few hours after sunset, you will see Hercules overhead and Scorpio low on the southern horizon. These are summer stars.

The star map was painted in reference to D(L)akota beadwork. It is said that each bead is a prayer. Beads are traditionally used to signify sacred items, such as medicine bags and pipe stems. Beadwork is also used to adorn clothing or accessories, like on an outfit to wear to a special occasion. Beaded items are worn with great pride, for example, a pow-wow outfit. The pinpoints of colorful dots in beadwork are reminiscent of starlight. The process of doing beadwork is meticulous and disciplined; it requires stillness. This stillness is echoed in the night sky. Beadwork and stars both sparkle.

The four directions are seen as spiritual and physical guideposts. Often seven directions are used, which include the four cardinal directions plus above, below, and center. Many ceremonies and everyday prayers use the directions to focus and send the prayers. Albert White Hat explains the four directions as *Tatuye topa,* the four winds. The cardinal direction North in particular is associated with the wintertime and stillness. Trees and plants appear "dead" on the outside in the winter, but they are still alive and growing on the inside, especially the roots. In wintertime, people follow this example. There is much stillness in the frozen terrain that is reflected in the northern stars, especially the motionless star, Polaris. Each of the solstices and equinoxes mark the beginning of a season and are considered sacred days and good times to pray and have ceremony. Albert White Hat explains, "The seasons are described as births. Every season is a new birth" [8].

Acknowledgements

The Native Skywatchers project acknowledges the elders and others who have kept this star knowledge alive. We acknowledge Paul Schultz (White Earth) who passed away suddenly in 2011 and Albert White Hat Sr. (Rosebud) who passed away in June 2013. Both men were collaborators with this project.

Funding to support this work has been provided by: NASA-Minnesota Space Grant, the Bush Foundation, Women's Foundation of Minnesota, NSF-North Star STEM Alliance, Minnesota State Arts Board, St. Cloud State University, and Fond du Lac Tribal and Community College. *Pidamaya/Pilamaya. Miigwech.* Thank you.

WAZIYATA WIÇAŊĦPI – NORTH CIRCUMPOLAR STARS

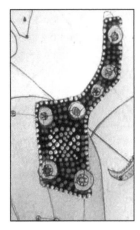

Fig. 10. To Wiŋ/Tuŋ Wiŋ

Fig. 9. "On the Wing"

To Wiŋ/Tuŋ Wiŋ – Blue Woman/Birth Woman – Big Dipper/Ursa Major

Midwives and others pray to the Blue/Birth Woman Spirit so newborn babies will enter this world safely. She is a doorkeeper between worlds.

Wiçakiyuhapi – Stretcher – Big Dipper/Bowl
Waṡihdapi/Waṡiglapi – Mourners – Big Dipper/Handle

The Stretcher carries a person that has passed away into the spirit world. These are the four stars on the bowl of the Big Dipper. The Mourners are the three handle stars that are carrying the deceased.

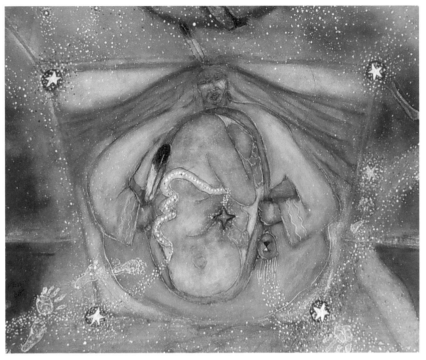

Fig. 11. Blue Woman-Birth Woman - Journey From the Stars

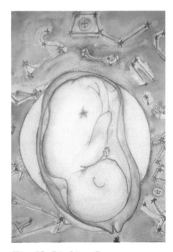

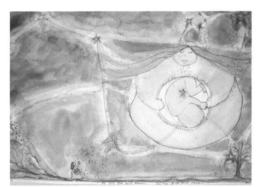

Fig. 12. Birthing Ceremony   *Fig. 13. Blue Spirit Woman*

Oçeti Śakowiŋ – Seven Sacred Rites/Council Fires – Big Dipper/Ursa Major

The Big Dipper also represents the *Oçeti Śakowin* – Seven Council Fires of the Dakota, Lakota, and Nakota nations.

Wiçakiyuhapi/Çançinśka – The Dipper/Wooden Spoon – Big Dipper/Ursa Major

Each year at sunrise on the Spring Equinox, the Big Dipper is part of the "Pipe Ceremony in the Stars."

Wiçaŋħpi Waziyata/Wiçaŋħpi Owaŋjila –
Star Which Stands in One Place – North Star/Polaris

According to Victor Douville (Rosebud Lakota), one story tells of how the

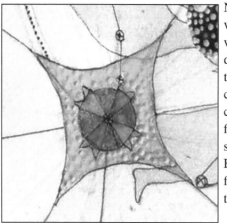

North Star married *Toŋwiŋ*, a human woman. She lived in the star world with him but missed her home. One day, she dug up a turnip (even though she was told not to), and this created a hole. Through this hole, she could see everyone back home. She fell through the hole. Her son survived and later became the hero, Fallen Star. North Star was so sad from losing his wife that he froze in the same spot [9].

Fig. 14. Wiçaŋħpi Waziyata/Wiçaŋħpi Owaŋjila – North Star

According to Madeline White (Sisseton Dakota), *Wiçaŋħpi Cekpa*, or Twin Star, is the mother of the Fallen Star hero. She and her beautiful twin sister both married handsome star men and were taken into the star world above. While there, she dug up a turnip, creating a hole through which she unsuccessfully tried to lower herself back down to Earth [10].

Wakiŋyaŋ – Thunderbird – Draco, Ursa Minor, and Precession Circle

The Thunderbird constellation lies at the center of the precession circle. The heart of the Thunderbird is the center of the circle. Because the Sun and Moon pull on the Earth, it wobbles like a top as it orbits. It is a small effect but noticeable over thousands of years. One complete wobble is 26,000 years; thus, while Polaris is above the North Pole today and for the next 1,000 years, its position will change. When the Egyptians built the pyramids 5,000 years ago, for example, the star Thuban (in our Thunderbird) served as the "North Star."

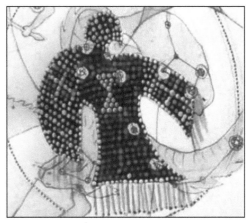

Fig. 15. Thunderbird

Fig. 16. Wakiŋyaŋ – Thunderbird Watching Over Us

9

Astronomical Treasures in the North – *Waziyata* – Circumpolar – All Seasons

Hubble Deep Fields

Over ten days in December 1995, the Hubble Space Telescope stared at a patch of dark sky the size of a grain of sand held at arm's length (2.5" across). In this speck of sky a 24-millionth of the entire sky, over 3,000 distinct galaxies were found. Many of these galaxies are the farthest and oldest objects ever seen by human eyes. These old galaxies appear smaller, more disturbed and irregular than those closer to us.

When looking far away in astronomy, we are actually looking back in time because of the time it takes light to travel across vast distances. We are looking back to nearly the beginning of the Universe (13.8 billion years ago) at galaxies roughly twelve billion years

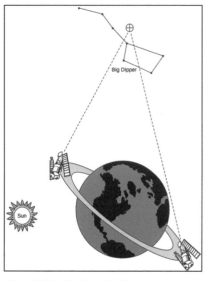

Fig. 17. Hubble Deep Field observing geometry

old. In 2004 and 2012, similar images were made with the Hubble Ultra-Deep Field and the Hubble Extreme Deep Field. Taking pictures within the constellation Fornax (below Orion) at exposure times of one-million and then two-million seconds (eleven days and twenty-two days), the Hubble cameras found 10,000 and 5,000 galaxies.

Delta Cephei

In one corner of the Greek constellation Cepheus the King, we see Delta Cephei, a star that appears noticeably dimmer over roughly a five-day period. As this dying star desperately tries to find balance, the outer layers are pulsing and expanding like a beating heart. The time it takes for the pattern to repeat, or period, can be correlated to how bright the star really is: The longer the period, the brighter the star. Using this information, we

Fig. 18. Hubble Deep Field

can find the distance to the star. Delta Cephei is called a "standard candle" and is useful to find distances. In the 1920s, Edwin Hubble found a Cepheid variable star in the Andromeda "Nebula" and was able to calculate its distance. This showed everyone that the Andromeda "Nebula" was actually outside of our Milky Way Galaxy, and it has ever since been called the Andromeda Galaxy.

Polaris, Thuban, and Precession

In D(L)akota, *Wiċaŋhpi Waziyata/ Wiċaŋhpi Owaŋjila* (Star Which Stands in One Place) is Polaris or the North Star. It

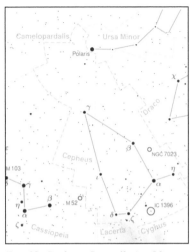

Fig. 19. Cepheus Constellation Map

is the only star in our sky that appears motionless, which is due to its current location less than 1° from the North Celestial Pole or Earth's northern rotational axis projected into space. An interesting point to keep in mind: due to the gravitational pull of the Sun and Moon on Earth, our rotational axis wobbles slightly. This can only be seen over thousands of years. Always about a 23.5-degree tilt from vertical, the axial tilt wobbles or processes in a circle in an approximately 26,000-year period. Consequently, Polaris will not always be the North Star. Twelve thousand years from now, the bright star Vega will be somewhat close to the North Celestial Pole. Of all the North Stars, Polaris is the brightest and closest to the North Celestial Pole. We are living in "The Age of Polaris."

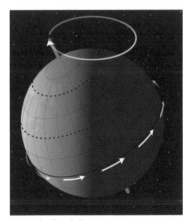

Fig. 20. Earth Precession

WIÇAŊĦPIWETU – SPRING STARS

Oçeti/Peta – Fireplace/Fire – Leo

The Fire/Fireplace constellation is the sacred fire built to heat the sacred stones for the sweat lodge ceremony. The Winter Circle is also seen as the Sweat Lodge/Womb in the stars and opens to face the direction of the Winter Circle/the Sweat Lodge. The journey of the incoming spirit follows the Road.

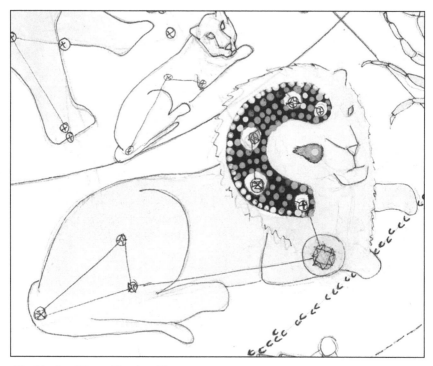

Fig. 21. Oçeti/Peta – Fireplace/Fire

Wiçaŋħpi Suŋkaku/Itkob u, Ihuku Kigle, Aŋpo Wiçaŋħpi Suŋkaku – Younger Brother of Morning Star/Going Toward/Under Went It – Arcturus (in Bootes)

This very bright star lies at the bottom of the Kite (Bootes). It can be found by following the bend in the handle of the Big Dipper and is seen overhead in the spring sky a few hours after sunset.

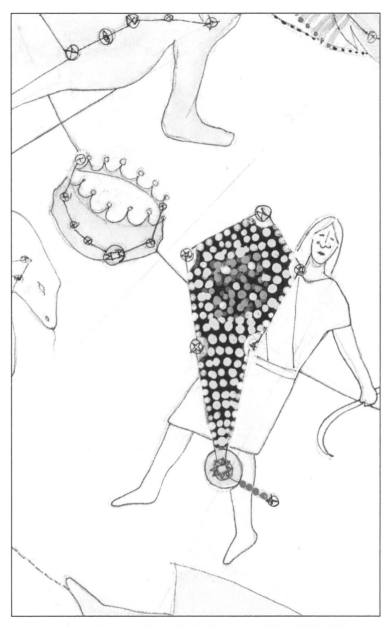

Fig. 22. Wiçaŋħpi Suŋkaku/Itkob u, Ihuku Kigle, Aŋpo Wiçaŋħpi Suŋkaku –
Younger Brother of Morning Star/Going Toward/Under Went It

Astronomical Treasures in *Wetu* – Spring

Fig. 23. Virgo Cluster

Virgo Cluster – Virgo

The bright star Spica lies at the bottom of the "y-shaped bowl" of Virgo, the maiden or virgin in Greek mythology. Inside the bowl is a cluster of galaxies called the "Virgo Cluster" containing some 1,300 galaxies [11]. This is the center of a larger object called the "Virgo Supercluster," of which the Local Group (and, therefore, the Milky Way) is a part. Incidentally, our cosmic address is:

Earth
Solar System
Milky Way Galaxy
Local Group
Virgo Supercluster
Universe

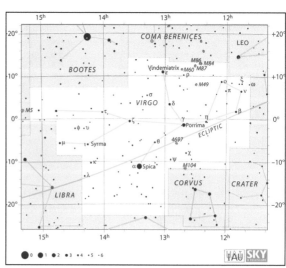

Fig. 24. Virgo Constellation

Fig. 25. Pipe Ceremony in the Stars

WIÇAŊHPI BDOKETU/BLOKETU – SUMMER STARS

Ahdeśka/Agleśka -Salamander – Cygnus

Fig. 26. Ahdeśka/Agleśka – Salamander
cord pouch

When a baby boy is born, the umbilical cord is cut from the mother and placed in a beaded leather pouch in the shape of the salamander. It is said that when the physical connection with the mother is severed, the connection to the stars is renewed. The salamander has characteristics of recovering from injury, agility and speed. Salamanders are similar to lizards but more closely associated with water. They are amphibians. (The young are aquatic, and the adults are semi-terrestrial.) Notice how *Ahdeśka/Agleśka* – Salamander is located in *Wanaǧi Taçaŋku* (Road of the Spirits/Ghost Trail) the Milky Way. The *kapemni* pair of the Milky Way is the Mississippi River.

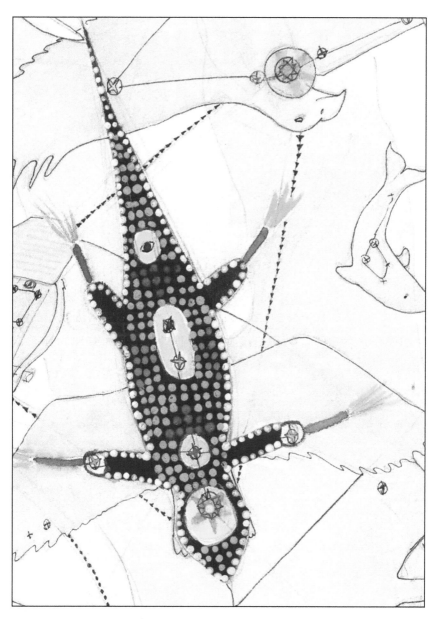

Fig. 27. Ahdeška/Agleška – Salamander

Astronomical Treasures in *Bdoketu/Bloketu* – Summer

Kepler Space Telescope

The Kepler Space telescope was launched in 2009 with the mission of determining how many other Earth-like (habitable) planets exist in our galaxy. It carefully observed over 145,000 stars while looking for a periodic dimming of starlight of roughly one part in 10,000. In an area the size of

Fig. 28. A Size Comparison of Exoplanets

a fist held at arm's length (10°x10°), between the Greek constellations Cygnus and Lyra, the Kepler telescope found 961 confirmed exoplanets and very possibly another 3,000 (as of February 2014). Using these data, it is now estimated that there are as many planets in our galaxy as there are stars: 100 - 400 billion planets [12]. It is also estimated there are forty billion Earth-sized planets orbiting in the habitable zone (the right conditions for liquid water) around their star in the Milky Way galaxy.

Hercules – M13 and Arecibo Message

In 1974, a radio message was sent towards the globular star cluster M13 in Hercules. Using only two digits, 0 and 1, a three-minute binary code message about humans was broadcast. The message contained some of the following information: numbers, atomic numbers of elements that make up DNA, the world population at the time, human dimensions, the telescope dimensions, and the layout of the solar system. The star cluster M13 contains over 300,000 densely packed stars in the constellation Hercules. Traveling at the speed of light, roughly 186,000 miles per second, it will take 25,000 years for the message to arrive at M13.

Fig. 29. Arecibo Message

Cygnus X-1

Also known as the Northern Cross, Cygnus the Swan contains one of the first-discovered stellar mass black holes. In 1964, astronomers found a strong x-ray source with no visible light counterpart coming from this position in the sky. Later research confirmed that Cygnus X-1 is part of an x-ray binary system. A large blue star, HDE 226868, is in a tight orbit with Cygnus X-1. The blue star is losing material to the black hole. As this stolen gas and dust hits the accretion disk of Cygnus X-1, it is heated to millions of degrees and shines in high energy x-rays.

Fig. 30. Black Hole (simulated)

M57, Ring Nebula

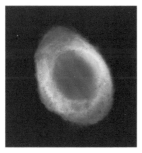

Fig. 31. Ring Nebula M57

The Ring Nebula, in the constellation Lyra the Harp (Greek mythology), is the last remnants of a dying star. Unlike massive stars that end their lives more dramatically, this middle mass star, after having exhausted all of its hydrogen fuel, expels its outer layers over tens of thousands of years, like a snake shedding its skin. The hot core of the star emits ultraviolet light, which ionizes the surrounding gas until it glows. The heavier elements, made only by stars, are recycled into space for the next generation of stars ("nucleosynthesis"). At the center of every planetary nebula is the compact core of a once healthy star. This object is called a "white dwarf"; with only electron pressure holding up against gravity, it is estimated that one teaspoon of white dwarf material weighs approximately ten tons [13].

Center of MWG, Supermassive Black Hole

Within the Greek constellation Sagittarius the Teapot is the direction to the center of the Milky Way Galaxy. Approximately 26,000 light years away, there is a supermassive black hole at the very center of the galaxy. Known as Sgr A*, it has a mass of roughly four million suns. This was calculated using Kepler/Newton's laws (derived in the 1600s) and watching the very fast orbits of nearby stars around the supermassive black hole. The orbital speeds of these very close stars tell us the mass of the central object.

Fig. 32. Sgr A*

WIÇAŊḢPI PTAŊYETU – FALL STARS

Keya – Turtle – Pegasus

When a baby girl is born, the umbilical cord is cut from the mother and placed in a beaded leather pouch in the shape of the turtle. It is said that when the physical connection with the mother is severed, the connection to the stars is renewed. The turtle carries its home on its back; it lives long with a strong heart and, therefore, is connected to wisdom and perseverance.

Fig. 33. Keya – Turtle Cord Pouch

Caŋsaśa Pusyapi/Ipusye – Dried Red Willow – Aries, Triangulum

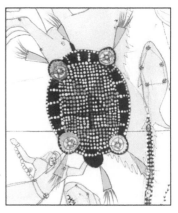

Fig. 34. Keya – Turtle

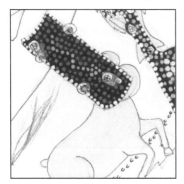

Fig. 35. Caŋsaśa Pusyapi/Ipusye – Dried Red Willow

The *Caŋsaśa Pusyapi/Ipusye* – Dried Red Willow constellation relates to one of the sacred plants used to pray with the pipe. The Red Willow constellation is seen at night in the fall, but the "Pipe Ceremony in the Stars" (see figure 25 above) happens each year at sunrise on the spring equinox as the Sun, the Red Willow constellation, and the Big Dipper line up along the eastern horizon.

Heȟaka/Upaη – Elk – Pisces

The Elk constellation is seen in the fall a few hours after sunset. This is the same time of the year that the elk lose their antlers to grow new ones ("rutting"). The elk constellation symbolizes love, romance, and fertility.

Wiçiηyaηna Śakowiη/Wiçiηcala Śakowiη – Seven Girls – Pleiades

The Seven Girls constellation tells a story about how seven small girls were taken from camp by a red eagle. The people could not kill the spirit bird, so they called on Fallen Star to save them. He placed the seven little girls in the night sky.

The Pleiades/Seven Girls constellation is also the Buffalo's head, *Tayamni pa.* Pleiades is seen overhead in late fall.

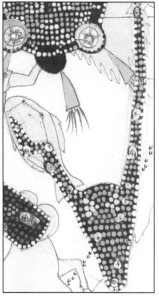

Fig. 36. Heȟaka/Upaη – Elk

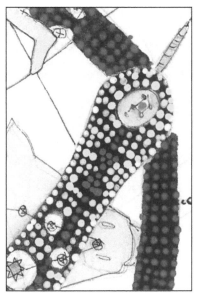

Fig. 37. Wiçiηyaηna Śakowiη/Wiçiηcala Śakowiη– Seven Girls – Pleiades

Fig. 38. Fall Stars

21

Astronomical Treasures in *Ptaŋyetu* – Fall

Fig. 39. Andromeda Galaxy M31

M31, Andromeda Galaxy

At a distance of 2.5 million light years (one light year is approximately 6 trillion miles), the Andromeda Galaxy is the farthest object that can be seen with the naked eye. A spiral galaxy containing about twice the number of stars as the Milky Way Galaxy (roughly one trillion stars) [14], it is the largest member of the Local Group. Gravity is pulling the two galaxies together, and we are on a collision course with our "sister spiral" that is estimated to happen in approximately four billion years. Individual stars are unlikely to collide, but the gas and dust will interact gravitationally causing both galaxies to merge, lose their spiral shape, and become one large elliptical galaxy.

Fig. 40. The Mice Galaxies NGC 4676

Pleiades/Seven Sisters

Fig. 41. Pleiades

Pleiades is a young (100 million years old) cluster of stars seen in the Greek constellation Taurus the Bull. Its most massive stars shine brightly in hot blue light, which is scattered efficiently by the surrounding dust in the area and causes the entire nebula to glow in blue light (called a "reflection nebula"). This cluster of about 1,000 stars will eventually disperse. Many indigenous cultures have star knowledge relating to the Pleiades star cluster. It is known as Seven Sisters (Greek mythology), as *Subaru* ("Unite") in Japan [15] and as *Dilyehe* ("Pinlike Sparkles") in Dine/Navajo [16].

Fomalhaut b

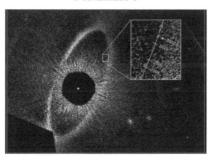

Fig. 42. Fomalhaut b

In 2008, using the Hubble Space Telescope, human beings photographed a direct image of another planet outside of our solar system for the first time. This planet orbits the star, Fomalhaut b, in the constellation Southern Pisces (Piscis Austrinus) about twenty-five light years away. The star system is very young, as indicated by the dusty accretion disk still in place around the central star. Fomalhaut b has an extremely wide orbit of 175 times the Earth-Sun distance and takes 2,000 years to complete one revolution.

WIÇAŊĦPI WANIYETU – WINTER STARS

Nape – Hand – Orion, Eridanus

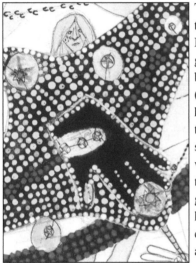

The *Nape* – Hand constellation refers to the story of the Chief who lost his hand. His trouble started when he stopped being generous and giving from his hand and became tired of sacrificing. The *Wakiŋyaŋ* (Thunderbeings) removed and hid his hand/arm in the sky. The constellation teaches the importance of generosity and sacrifice as part of the balance of life. The word *waçaŋtohnaka* means "from within the heart" and modeling extreme generosity, which the Chief failed to do for his people and for which he felt the consequences that we still see semi-annually in the stars.

Fig. 43. Nape – Hand

Maţo Tipi/Maţo Tipila – Bear's Lodge – Gemini

The *Maţo Tipi/Maţo Tipila* constellation is connected with the Bear and is seen overhead in the winter a few hours after sunset. The Bear's Lodge is paired with/mirrors the sacred site *Pŧe He Gi*– Grey Horn Butte/Grey Buffalo Horn – Devil's Tower. Traditionally, *Wi Waŋyaŋka Waçipi,* the Sundance ceremony, was held at Grey Horn Butte during the season when this constellation is overhead during the day, i.e., summertime, particularly the summer solstice.

The Bear is strong and smart and helps lead us to the medicine plants. They are four-legged and, sometimes, two-legged like us.

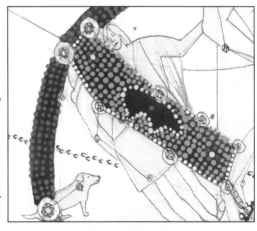

Fig. 44. Maţo Tipi/Maţo Tipila – Bear's Lodge

Ki Iŋyaŋka Oçaŋku – Racetrack/Winter Circle, expanded to include Pleiades

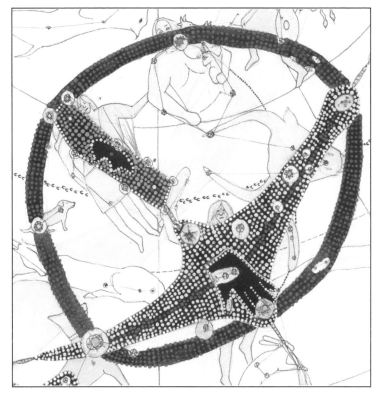

Fig. 45. Ki Iŋyaŋka Oçaŋku – Racetrack

The Racetrack constellation is tied to the story of the Great Race between the four legged and the winged-ones to determine the fate of the two-legged (humans). The sacred racetrack can be seen in the red clay surrounding *Paha Saṗa* – the Black Hills. The red color is the blood trail of the animals in the race.

The Black Hills is also known as the "Heart of Everything that Is." As seen from this satellite image of the Black Hills, as viewed from space, it does appear in the shape of a heart and has red clay/soil encircling the area.

Fig. 46. Satellite image of Black Hills, SD

Çaŋ Hd/Gleška Wakaŋ – Sacred Hoop/Winter Circle,
expanded to include Pleiades

Another constellation in the same area of sky as the *Ki Iŋyaŋka Oçaŋku* –
Racetrack is the *Çaŋ Hd/Gleška Wakaŋ* – the Sacred Hoop. This refers to the
large circular shape as a womb. It is seen as a womb because the *Tayamni* –
Buffalo Embryo constellation is within it.

Inipi/Initipi – Sweat Lodge/Winter Circle, expanded to include Pleiades
Tayamni – Buffalo (four parts of) – Orion, Canis Major, Pleiades

The *Tayamni* constellation is a spirit animal that has characteristics of a buffalo
embryo. There are four parts: *Tayamni Pa* – the head, *Tayamni Çaŋkahu* – the
backbone, *Tayamni Tuçuhu/Çutuhu* – the ribs, and *Tayamni Siŋte* – the tail. The
head is the Pleiades open star cluster. The backbone corresponds to Orion's Belt
stars. The ribs are formed by connecting the backbone to Betelgeuse on the left
and Rigel on the right. The brightest star in the night sky, Sirius, marks *Tayamni
Siŋte* – the tail.

The buffalo embryo emerges from the Sacred Hoop or Womb constellation –
Winter Circle. Notice how the *Wanaġi Taçaŋku* – Road of the Spirits/Ghost
Trail, the Milky Way goes directly through the center of the Womb. The
teaching is that the spirit comes from the Star World through the *Wanaġi
Taçaŋku* – Road of the Spirits/Ghost Trail and then emerges from the Womb
going to *Oçeti/Peta* – Fireplace/Fire in Leo. After the purification ceremony,
Inipi, the spirit, meets with *To Wiŋ/Tuŋ Wiŋ* – Blue Woman/Birth Woman at the
doorway between above and below at the scoop of the Big Dipper.

Zuzeca/Zuzuheça – Snake – Columbia, Puppis, Canis Major

The snake is sometimes portrayed as swallowing an egg, which represents
protecting the culture. The snake constellation may be represented on earth by
the Serpentine Mounds in Ohio or other similar mounds. Jim Rock sees this
constellation intended as the serpent drawings in *Wakaŋ Tipi* cave on the
Mississippi River in St. Paul, Minnesota.

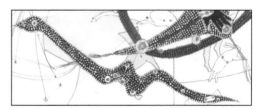

Fig. 47. Zuzeca/Zuzuheça – Snake

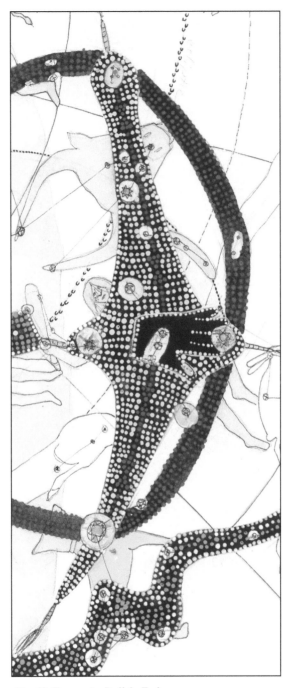

Fig. 48. Tayamni – Buffalo Embryo

Astronomical Treasures in *Waniyetu* – Winter

Fig. 49. Orion Nebula M42

M42, The Orion Nebula

In the area below the belt of Orion is a fuzzy patch of sky that is visible on a dark clear night with the naked eye. This is the Great Orion Nebula. Over 1,000 light years away, this huge area of star formation is twenty-four light years across. Using the Hubble Space Telescope, we have zoomed in to see newly forming stars complete with their proplanetary discs. For the first time in human history, we have taken images of distant "solar systems" forming. One of the things that the Orion Nebula teaches us is that planetary systems appear to be common.

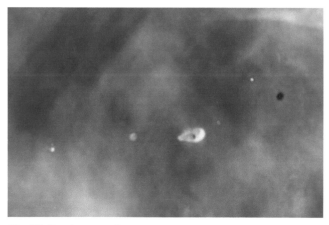

Fig. 50. Proplanetary discs

Crab SNR

In the Greek constellation Taurus the Bull is the leftover cloud of a massive star that ran out of fuel and exploded in the form of a type II supernova. The Chinese and others recorded this event in 1054 AD. These violent explosions are the only known process in the universe to make most atoms. We are made of star stuff [17]. Western science calls this process "nucleosynthesis." Jim Rock notes that nucleosynthesis is another appropriate interpretation of the D/Lakota *Otokahekagapi* story.

What remains of the original star after the supernova explosion is one of the most compact objects known, a neutron star. The incredible pull of gravity is balanced only by quantum mechanical pressure from the neutrons. One teaspoon of neutron star weighs about 100 million tons [18]. This particular neutron star is spinning about thirty times around in one second. Its poles are directly toward our line of sight, and we receive a radio pulse from it every thirty-three milliseconds. The pulsar star is about the size of a small city (twelve miles in diameter).

Fig. 51. Crab Pulsar M1

At the top left shoulder of the Orion constellation in Greek mythology is Betelgeuse, a star in its last moments of life. As it struggles to find balance after running out of its main fuel, hydrogen, the outer layers swell up, and the star cools in temperature. Betelgeuse is a reddish color star. If we replaced Betelguese with the Sun, its outer layers would extend past the orbit of Mars. The Earth would be inside the swollen, dying star. Our Sun is expected to become a red giant in about 4.5 billion years. Compare this red, cool star with the bluish star called "Rigel" at the bottom right in Orion. Rigel is also a dying star, but nuclear processes have allowed it to maintain a very high temperature, about twice the temperature of the Sun (about 20,000 degrees Fahrenheit) [19].

VENUS

Fig. 52. Venus: visible wavelengths (left), radar (right)

Venus is the third brightest object in the sky after the Sun and the Moon. It is so bright that it is often mistaken for a UFO because Venus is the closest planet to us at roughly twenty-five million miles (compared to Mars at forty-seven million miles at closest approach). Its brightness is due to light reflected from the Sun; like Earth and all terrestrial planets, Venus does not generate any visible light. Venus' light is especially bright because it is covered in white, reflective clouds. For this reason, people in the early twentieth century had a fascination with "life on Venus" because we could not see what was underneath the sulfuric acid clouds. In the 1960s, the first missions used radar wavelengths

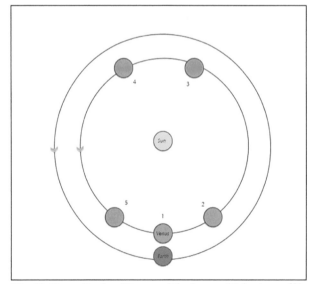

Fig. 53. Venus-Earth orbit around the Sun, multiple views of Venus in orbit

to cut through the cloud layer and see the topography underneath. We found extensive volcanism [20]. At one time, Venus could have had oceans, but due to the runaway greenhouse effect, Venus is now the hottest planet in the Solar System (~800 °F). The heat, combined with the shutdown of Venus' magnetic field, would have caused the water molecules to separate into hydrogen and oxygen ("photodissociation") and the hydrogen atoms to be stripped away by the solar wind [21]. Despite its desert-like volcanic surface, Venus is closest to Earth in size, density, and gravity and is nicknamed Earth's "Sister planet."

D(L)akota Connection to Venus

In D(L)akota, the word for Venus is *Aŋpetu D/Luta,* which translates "Red Day Star" [22]. This idea has several layers. The first understanding is literal. The "star-like" point of light that is the planet Venus, and the surrounding sky, appear reddish in color because Venus can only be seen low on the eastern or western horizon at sunrise or sunset. When celestial objects are positioned low in the sky (or just above the horizon), they appear reddish. This is due to Rayleigh scattering. The longer path of sunlight through the atmosphere at low elevations removes almost all blue and green light.

Another layer of meaning in *Aŋpetu D/Luta Wiçaŋħpi* – Red Day Star requires a cultural context. Red is a sacred color; to say a "red day" is equivalent to "a sacred day." For example, a traditional D(L)akota person wakes up and gives thanks for life and the chance to live another day. Recently, people refer to walking on the "red road." It is a way of remembering our connection with all living beings, also stated as *mitakuye oyasin/owasiŋ* – all my relatives. *Aŋpetu*

Fig. 54. Scattering of Sunlight at Sunset

D/Luta Wiçaŋhpi – Red Day Star is considered one of the leaders of the star nation. All families with the name D/Luta – Red were keepers of the star knowledge, for example: Red Eagle, Red Deer, Red Willow, Red Horse, Red Day, and so on. These families traditionally protected and passed down the star knowledge from generation to generation. Furthermore, traditional star quilts were made with one large star in the center; this was in honor of *Aŋpetu D/Luta Wiçaŋhpi* – Red Day Star [23].

Another word for morning star is *Aŋpo Wiçaŋhpi* or *Aŋpao Wiçaŋhpi*. This refers to dawn or "as the morning comes" [24]. In this context, *Aŋpo Wiçaŋhpi* specifically refers to Venus as the Morning Star as opposed to *Wiçaŋhpi Haŋyetu* or *Haŋyetu Wiçaŋhpi,* the Evening Star. Note that the star Arcturus in the Greek constellation Bootes is called *Aŋpo Suŋkaku Wiçaŋhpi,* which means Younger Brother of Morning Star.

Fig. 55. Star Quilt

Cycles of Venus

Position	Phase of Venus	Other comments/names associated with this position
1	New	Not visible, also called "Inferior Conjunction."
1-2	Waxing Crescent	Not visible
2	Waxing Crescent	Venus first visible in the East before sunrise, called the "Morning Star."
2-3	Moving from Waxing Crescent through First Quarter to Waxing Gibbous	Venus is seen as the Morning Star for about 9 months.
3	Waxing Gibbous	The last day that Venus is visible as the Morning Star.
3-4	Moving from Waxing Gibbous to Full (directly in line with the Earth-Sun) to Waning Gibbous	Not visible
4	Waning Gibbous	Venus first visible in the West at Sunset, called the "Evening Star."
4-5	Moving from Waning Gibbous through Last Quarter to Waning Crescent	Venus is seen as the Evening Star for about 9 months.
5	Waning Crescent	The last day that Venus is visible as the Evening Star.
5-1	Moving from Waning Crescent to New, the cycle repeats.	Not visible

Fig. 56. Lunar Eclipse

MOON

Traditionally, the Dakota/Lakota used the Sun, Moon, and stars to keep track of the passing of time. They used the seasons and the activities that were culturally significant each month. The word "month" is derived from *moneth,* which comes from "moon" [25]. The moon takes 29.5 days to make one circle around the Earth as seen from our backyard. Today, we can make a calendar with twelve months and correlate what the D(L)akota months would be. Traditionally, the D(L)akota lunar calendar starts in spring and sometimes has an extra moon or month in winter.

The name of the moon each month signifies whatever is happening that is important to survival, gathering of food, or a unique characteristic of that time. This method of time keeping denotes the priority of the actual event and not an abstract construction of a time-keeping device. For example, June is *Wažuśtecaśa Wi* – Strawberry Ripening Moon, or in Lakota, it is *Wipazuka*

Waste Wi – Moon of Good Berries; it is the time of the year when the berries are ripe. It is the only time of year when it happens; if you miss out, you have to wait until next year to gather strawberries or hope to trade with someone for berries. Paying attention to when the food is ready is crucial for survival.

Also different from Western timekeeping is that the names of the moon change with location. This could be because of different climates at different latitudes or different topography at different longitudes. For example, October is known by Dakota as *Wi Wažupi* – Drying Rice Moon, but in Lakota country wild rice does not grow (plains topography, not wetlands); the Lakota October moon is *Caŋwahpekasna Wi* – Trees Shaking Off the Leaves Moon.

People kept track of time using the phases of the Moon and the lunar calendar. For example, someone would say, "I was born on the full moon during the *Wožupi Wi* – Planting Moon" or would express age as "My grandchildren have grandchildren" (approximately 80 years old).

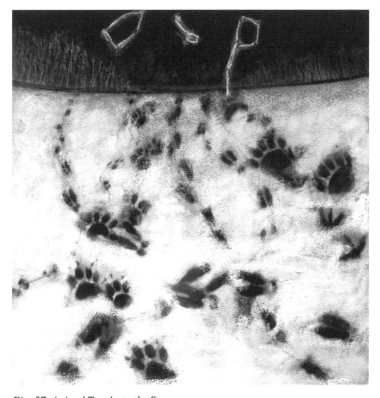

Fig. 57. Animal Tracks to the Stars

CONCLUSION

The work presented here is interdisciplinary: astronomy, culture, art, and language are each represented. The delivery of an in-depth, interdisciplinary topic like indigenous astronomy can be overwhelming to students, adults, or youth who have grown up with light pollution, tall buildings, and computers. Unlike traditional native people, today we tend to spend a lot of time indoors. Most people, however, have at least some familiarity with the Big Dipper, Sun, and Moon. The delivery of this culturally rich material must be simple, yet allow for complexity and abstraction. To achieve this goal, we first use the cultural framework of the four directions. The current night sky is subdivided into North, East, South/overhead, and West; thus, from the beginning of the discussion, the cultural context is intact. The four directions are considered an important framework and guideposts in native culture. This instructional approach builds on a sense of place [26] and allows participants to orientate the current night sky with the cardinal directions. The technique grounds the complexity of the current night sky in the tangible and the simple, yet creates a multi-layered, circular learning approach. Following this approach allows for the widest range of participants to take part in the learning experience.

Furthermore, the stars and constellations can be best understood in terms of the four seasons. The discussion is simplified again by fixing the time as a few hours after sunset. This is the observing time and is referred to as "prime time" for stargazing. Only in the northern direction will the circumpolar stars, or northern stars as seen from approximately 45-55° N latitude/85-110° W longitude, be visible throughout the year. When an observer faces due South (azimuth 180° along the horizon), he/she will see the current season of stars. The previous season will be seen setting in the West and the following season will be seen rising in the East. The *Makoçe Wiçaŋĥpi Wowapi* – D(L)akota Star Map is best presented by transforming the discussion into an experiential, hands-on event. In addition, this highly visual, holistic, and cooperative learning environment is consistent with a traditional native learning style [27].

Finally, we encourage mindfulness of cultural protocols. Native knowledge is sometimes a different way of knowing than Western science. There are strict cultural protocols that must be respected, such as when some stories are to be told; for example, some are only told when there is snow on the ground. We must be extremely careful not to introduce or propagate error into the written or oral records. Use caution and be hesitant. Users of these materials are urged to seek out elders and native community members to bring into the classroom. Materials represented here should be viewed as a beginning.

Pidamaya/Pilamaya. Miigwech. Thank you.

Fig. 58. Building Community Around the Native Star Knowledge

APPENDIX

D(L)AKOTA MONTHS/MOONS: MINNESOTA & SOUTH DAKOTA [28]

Month	Dakota/Lakota	English
January	*Witehi Wi/ Wiot' ehika Wi/Çaŋkapopa Wi*	Hard/Difficult Moon/Tree Popping Moon
February	*Wiçaṭ' a Wi /Aŋpetu Numnuŋpa Wi/Wicata Wi/Cannapopa Wi*	Raccoon Moon/Moon When Many Die/ Two Different Kinds of Days Moon/Moon of Popping Trees
March	*Išta Wicayazaŋ Wi*	Sore Eyes Moon
April	*Watopapi Wi/ Maġa Okada Wi/ Wokada Wi/ Wihakakta Wi*	Moon When Streams Are Open/Goose Egg-Laying Moon/Egg Laying Moon/Moon of Fattening
May	*Wożupi Wi*	Planting Moon
June	*Ważuštecaśa Wi/Wipazuka Waste Wi*	Strawberry Ripening Moon/ Moon of Good Berries
July	*Çaŋpasapa Wi/Çaŋpaśa Wi/Waśuŋpa Wi*	Moon When the Chokecherries Are Ripe (Black)/"/Moon When the Geese Shed Their Feathers
August	*Wasutuŋ Wi*	Harvest Moon
September	*Psiŋhnaketu Wi/Taśaheca Hakita Wi/ Wayuksapi Wi/ Canwapegi Wi*	Moon When the Rice is Laid-up to Dry/ Moon When the Chipmunk Looks Back/Corn Harvesting Moon/Moon of Brown Leaves
October	*Çaŋwahpekasna Wi/Wi Ważupi/*	Trees Shaking off the Leaves Moon/Drying Rice Moon
November	*Takiyuha Wi/ Waniyetu Wi*	Deer Rutting Moon/Moon of Rutting Deer
December	*Tahecapśuŋ Wi*	Deer Antler Shedding Moon

D(L)AKOTA CELESTIAL VOCABULARY

	Dakota/Lakota	**Related Greek Constellations**
***WANIYETU* - WINTER**		
Hand	*Nape*	Orion, Eridanus
Bear's Lodge	*Maṭo Tipi/Maṭo Tipila*	Gemini
Racetrack	*Ki Iŋyaŋka Oçaŋku*	Winter Circle
Sacred Hoop	*Çaŋ Hd/Gleśka Wakaŋ*	Winter Circle
Sweat Lodge	*Inipi/Initipi*	Winter Circle
Buffalo (four parts of)	*Tayamni*	Orion, Canis Major, Pleiades
Snake	*Zuzeca/Zuzuheça*	Columbia, Puppis, Canis Major
***WAZIYATA* - NORTH**		
Blue Woman/ Birth Woman	*To Win/Tuŋ Wiŋ*	Big Dipper - Inside Bowl
Stretcher	*Wiçakiyuhapi*	Big Dipper - Bowl stars
Mourners	*Waśihdapi/Waśiglapi*	Big Dipper - Handle stars
Skunk	*Maŋka/Maka*	Big Dipper
The Dipper/ Wooden Spoon	*Wicakiyuhapi/ Can cinkska*	Big Dipper
Seven Sacred Rites/ Council Fires	*Oçeti Śakowiŋ*	Big Dipper
North star	*Wiçaŋħpi Waziyata/ Wiçaŋħpi Owaŋjila (Star Which Stands in One Place)*	Polaris
Thunderbird	*Wakiŋyaŋ*	Draco, Ursa Minor
***PTAŊYETU* - FALL**		
Turtle	*Keya*	Pegasus
Dried Red Willow	*Caŋśaśa Pusyapi/Ipusye*	Aries, Triangulum
Elk	*Heħaka/Upaŋ*	Pisces
Seven Girls	*Wiçiŋyaŋna Śakowiŋ/ Wiçiŋcala Śakowiŋ*	Pleiades
***BDOKETU/BLOKETU* - SUMMER**		
Salamander	*Ahdeśka/Agleśka*	Cygnus
WETU - SPRING		
Fireplace/Fire	*Oçeti/Peta*	Leo
Arcturus (bright star in Bootes)	*Itkob u (Going Toward), Ihuku Kigle (Under Went It), Aŋpo Wiçaŋħpi Suŋkaku (Younger Brother of Morning Star)*	

OTHER CELESTIAL VOCABULARY	
Star	*Wiçaŋhpi*
Star Nation	*Wiçaŋhpi Oyate*
Moon	*Haŋhepi Wi /Haŋyetu Wi/Haŋwi /Haŋwi (Night Sun)*
Moon	*Anog Ite (Double Faced Woman)*
Sun	*Wi, Aŋpetu Wi (Day Sun)*
Venus - Morning Star	*Aŋpo Wiçaŋhpi /Aŋpetu D/Luta*
Ecliptic	*Çaŋku Wiçaŋhpi Omani/Mahpiya Maka Iciyagle*
Milky Way (MW)	*Wanaği Taçaŋku (Road of the Spirits/Ghost Trail)*
Meteor/Falling Star	*Wiçaŋhpi Hiŋhpaya/ Wiahpihinhpaya/Wohpe Wakaŋ*
Universe	*Wamakohnaka/Wamakhognaka/ Makasitomni*
Aurora Borealis (Northern Lights)	*Wanaği Tawaçipi (Spirit Dancers)/ Mahpiyataŋiŋ/Wiyosaya*
Comet	*Wiçaŋhpi Siŋtetuŋ/Wiçaŋhpi Siŋte Yukan/ Wicaŋpisiŋtetoŋ*
Star map	*Makoçe Wiçaŋhpi Wowapi*
Planet	*Wiçaŋhpi Omani/Wiçaŋhpi Nuni/Wiçaŋhpi Sa*
Sundogs	*Wiaceic' iti (Sun Making Fire)*
Solar Eclipse	*Witha Wit' e (Sun Dies)*
Lunar Eclipse	*Haŋwitha*
Constellations	*Wiçaŋhpi Tiospaye (Extended Family)*
Galaxies	*Okakše Taŋka Wiçaŋhpi Ota/Wiçaŋhpi Optaye Taŋka*
Groups of galaxies	*Wiçaŋhpi Oyate (Nation)*

OTHER CELESTIAL VOCABULARY	
Summer Solstice	*Bdoke cokaya/Bloke cokaya/Anpawi (Morning Sun)*
Winter Solstice	*Waniyetu cokaya/Nahomni (Swing Around)*
Spring Equinox	*Wetu Aŋpa Haŋyetu Iyehaŋtu*
Fall Equinox	*Ptaŋyetu Aŋpa Haŋyetu Iyehaŋtu*
Seasons	*Omaka/Makoncage (Earth Grows with Time Change)*
North	*Waziyata*
South	*Itokagata*
East	*Wiohinyanpata*
West	*Wiyohpeyata*
Above	*Wankantu/Waŋkatika*
Below	*Kutakiya/Kutkiya*
Center	*Çokata/Çokaya*
Buffalo embryo head	*Tayamni pa* (Pleiades)
Buffalo embryo ribs	*Tayamni cutuhu* (Betelgeuse and Rigel)
Buffalo embryo backbone	*Tayamni caŋkahu* (Orion's Belt)
Buffalo embroy tail	*Tayamni siŋte* (Sirius)

FIGURES

Fig. 1. *Makoče Wiçaŋḣpi Wowapi – D(L)akota Star Map.* Annette S. Lee and Jim Rock. Watercolor and mixed media on paper, 36 x 36," 2012.

Fig. 2. *Kapemni.* Illustration created by Annette S. Lee, 2009.

Fig. 3. *Pte He Ġi, Grey Horn Butte/Grey Buffalo Horn.* Photo by Annette S. Lee, 2011.

Fig. 4. *Wakaŋ Tipi Cave,* St. Paul, MN. From the original inventory of the Robert N. Dennis collection of stereoscopic views. Retrieved May 2014 from <http://commons.wikimedia.org/wiki/File:Carver's_cave,_near_St._Paul,_Minn,_from_Robert_N._Dennis_collection_of_stereoscopic_views.png>.

Fig. 5. *Cottonwood tree in winter.* Photo by Annette S. Lee, 2010.

Fig. 6. *Cottonwood leaves in summer.* Photo by Annette S. Lee, 2009.

Fig. 7. *Cross-section of cottonwood branch, "Star Tree."* Photo by Annette S. Lee, 2009.

Fig. 8. *Makoče Wiçaŋḣpi Wowapi– D(L)akota Star Map.* Annette S. Lee and Jim Rock. Watercolor and mixed media on paper, 36 x 36," 2012.

Fig. 9. *On the Wing.* Photo of north circumpolar stars and northern lights by Ian Bernick, 2012.

Fig. 10. *To Win/Tuŋ Wiŋ - Blue Woman/Birth Woman.* Close up from *Makoče Wiçaŋḣpi Wowapi– D(L)akota Star Map,* by Annette S. Lee and Jim Rock. Watercolor and mixed media on paper, 36 x 36," 2012.

Fig. 11. *To/Tuŋ Wiŋ (Birth/Blue Spirit Woman) - Journey From the Stars.* Annette S. Lee. Oil and mixed media on panel, 2014.

Fig. 12. *Birthing Ceremony - We Come From the Stars.* Annette S. Lee. Watercolor and mixed media on paper, 2010.

Fig. 13. *Blue Spirit Woman.* Annette S. Lee. Watercolor and mixed media on paper, 2008.

Fig. 14. *North Star.* Close up from *Makoče Wiçaŋḣpi Wowapi – D(L)akota Star Map,* by Annette S. Lee and Jim Rock. Watercolor and mixed media on paper, 36 x 36," 2012.

Fig. 15. *Thunderbird.* Close up from *Makoče Wiçaŋḣpi Wowapi – D(L)akota Star Map,* by Annette S. Lee and Jim Rock. Watercolor and mixed media on paper, 36 x 36," 2012.

Fig. 16. *Wakiŋyaŋ (Thunderbird) and Caŋcega (Drum).* Annette S. Lee. Oil and mixed media on panel, 2014.

Fig. 17. *Hubble Deep Field Observing Geometry.* NASA image public domain. 2007.

Fig. 18. *Hubble Deep Field (full mosaic).* NASA image public domain. 1996.

Fig. 19. *Cepheus Constellation Map.* IAU and Sky & Telescope Magazine (Roger Sinnott and Rick Fienberg), 2011.

Fig. 20. *Earth Precession.* NASA, Vectorized by Mysid in Inkscape after a

NASA Earth Observatory image in Milutin Milankovitch Precession.

Fig. 21. *Oçeti/Peta - Fireplace/Fire.* Close up from *Makoçe Wiçaŋhpi Wowapi – D(L)akota Star Map,* by Annette S. Lee and Jim Rock. Watercolor and mixed media on paper, 36 x 36," 2012.

Fig. 22. *Wiçaŋhpi Suŋkaku /Itkob u, Ihuku Kigle, Aŋpo Wiçaŋhpi Suŋkaku - Younger Brother of Morning Star/Going Toward/Under Went It.* Close up from *Makoçe Wiçaŋhpi Wowapi– D(L)akota Star Map,* by Annette S. Lee and Jim Rock. Watercolor and mixed media on paper, 36 x 36," 2012.

Fig. 23. *Virgo Cluster.* Chris Mihos (Case Western Reserve University)/ESO, 2009.

Fig. 24. *Virgo constellation.* IAU and Sky & Telescope Magazine (Roger Sinnott & Rick Fienberg), 2011.

Fig. 25. *Pipe Ceremony in the Stars.* Painting by Annette S. Lee. Watercolor and mixed media, 10 x 18," 2011.

Fig. 26. *Ahdeśka/Agleśka Cord Bag.* Created and photographed by Annette S. Lee.

Fig. 27. *Ahdeśka/Agleśka – Salamander.* Close up from *Makoçe Wiçaŋhpi Wowapi – D(L)akota Star Map,* by Annette S. Lee and Jim Rock. Watercolor and mixed media on paper, 36 x 36," 2012.

Fig. 28. *A size comparison of the exoplanets Kepler-20e and Kepler-20f with Venus and Earth.* NASA/Ames/JPL-Caltech, Public domain.

Fig. 29. *Arecibo Message.* Sent 1974 from the Arecibo Observatory, Arne Nordmann, 2005.

Fig. 30. *Black Hole.* Simulated view of a black hole in front of the Large Magellanic Cloud, Alain r, 2006.

Fig. 31. *Ring nebula M57.* The Hubble Heritage Team (AURA/STScI/NASA), 1998.

Fig. 32. *Sgr A*. Chandra (x-ray) image.* Based on data from one million seconds or almost two weeks, NASA/CXC/MIT/F. Baganoff, R. Shcherbakov et al., 2010.

Fig. 33. *Cord bag – Keya.* Made by and photographed by C. O'Rourke, 2014.

Fig. 34. *Keya-Turtle.* Close up from *Makoçe Wiçaŋhpi Wowapi – D(L)akota Star Map,* by Annette S. Lee and Jim Rock. Watercolor and mixed media on paper, 36 x 36," 2012.

Fig. 35. *Caŋśaśa Pusyapi/Ipusye – Dried Red Willow.* Close up from *Makoçe Wiçaŋhpi Wowapi– D(L)akota Star Map,* by Annette S. Lee and Jim Rock. Watercolor and mixed media on paper, 36 x 36," 2012.

Fig. 36. *Heĥaka/Upaŋ – Elk.* Close up from *Makoçe Wiçaŋhpi Wowapi– D(L)akota Star Map,* by Annette S. Lee and Jim Rock. Watercolor and mixed media on paper, 36 x 36," 2012.

Fig. 37. *Tayamni pa - Buffalo's head - Pleiades.* Close up from *Makoçe*

Wiçaŋhpi Wowapi– D(L)akota Star Map, by Annette S. Lee and Jim Rock. Watercolor and mixed media on paper, 36 x 36," 2012.

Fig. 38. *Fall Stars.* Annette S. Lee. Oil and mixed media on panel, 2013.

Fig. 39. *Andromeda Galaxy M31.* Adam Evans, 2010, Creative Commons, <http://en.wikipedia.org/wiki/Andromeda_Galaxy#mediaviewer/File:A ndromeda_Galaxy_(with_h-alpha).jpg>.

Fig. 40. *The Mice Galaxies NGC4676.* NASA, H. Ford (JHU), G. Illingworth (UCSC/LO), M. Clampin (STScI), G. Hartig (STScI), the ACS Science Team, and ESA, 2002.

Fig. 41. *Pleiades M45.* NASA, ESA, AURA/Caltech, Palomar Observatory, 2004.

Fig. 42. *Fomalhaut b.* NASA and ESA, 2013.

Fig. 43. *Nape – Hand.* Close up from *Makoçe Wiçaŋhpi Wowapi – D(L)akota Star Map,* by Annette S. Lee and Jim Rock. Watercolor and mixed media on paper, 36 x 36," 2012.

Fig. 44. *Maṭo Tipi/Maṭo Tipila – Bear's Lodge.* Close up from *Makoçe Wiçaŋhpi Wowapi – D(L)akota Star Map,* by Annette S. Lee and Jim Rock. Watercolor and mixed media on paper, 36 x 36," 2012.

Fig. 45. *Ki Iŋyaŋka Oçaŋku – Racetrack, Çaŋ Hd/Gleṡka Wakaŋ - Sacred Hoop, Inipi/Initipi – Sweat Lodge.* Close up from *Makoçe Wiçaŋhpi Wowapi – D(L)akota Star Map,* by Annette S. Lee and Jim Rock. Watercolor and mixed media on paper, 36 x 36," 2012.

Fig. 46. *Black Hills.* Satellite image with shaded relief map of Black Hills in southwest South Dakota, U. S. Geological Survey – USGS.

Fig. 47. *Zuzeca/Zuzuheça – Snake.* Close up from *Makoçe Wiçaŋhpi Wowapi– D(L)akota Star Map,* by Annette S. Lee and Jim Rock. Watercolor and mixed media on paper, 36 x 36," 2012.

Fig. 48. *Tayamni – Buffalo Embryo.* Close up from *Makoçe Wiçaŋhpi Wowapi – D(L)akota Star Map,* by Annette S. Lee and Jim Rock. Watercolor and mixed media on paper, 36 x 36," 2012.

Fig. 49. *Orion Nebula M42.* NASA, ESA, M. Robberto (Space Telescope Science Institute/ESA) and the Hubble Space Telescope Orion Treasury Project Team, 2006.

Fig. 50. *M42 Proplyds.* C.R. O'Dell/Rice University; NASA, public domain, <http://en.wikipedia.org/wiki/Orion_nebula#mediaviewer/File:M42pro plyds.jpg>.

Fig. 51. *Crab Pulsar M1.* Composite image of x-ray (blue) and optical (red) images superimposed, Optical: NASA/HST/ASU/J. Hester et al. X-Ray: NASA/CXC/ASU/J. Hester et al., 2002.

Fig. 52. *Venus: Visible wavelengths (left)/Radar (right).* Photo courtesy of NASA.

Fig. 53. *Diagram of Venus Phases.* Top view of Sun-Earth-Venus system.

Created by Annette S. Lee, 2014.

REFERENCES

1. Morton, R. and Gawboy, C. 2003. *Talking Rocks: Geology and 10,000 Years of Native American Tradition in the Lake Superior Region.* Minneapolis: University of Minnesota Press.
2. Goodman, R. 1992. *Lakota Star Knowledge: Studies in Lakota Stellar Theology.* Mission: Sinte Gleska University.
3. P. Schultz, Personal Communication.
4. Minnesota Department of Education. 2010, "Minnesota Academic Standards—Science K-12." Retrieved from <http://education.state.mn.us/MDE/EdExc/StanCurri/K-12AcademicStandards/index. htm>.
5. Goodman, R. 1992. *Lakota Star Knowledge: Studies in Lakota Stellar Theology.* Mission SD: Sinte Gleska University.
6. Goodman, R. 1992. *Lakota Star Knowledge: Studies in Lakota Stellar Theology.* Mission SD: Sinte Gleska University.
7. Goodman, R. 1992. *Lakota Star Knowledge: Studies in Lakota Stellar Theology.* Mission SD: Sinte Gleska University.
8. White Hat Sr., A. 1999. *Reading and Writing the Lakota Language.* Salt Lake City: University of Utah Press, 93-94.
9. Victor Douville, Personal Communication. Sinte Gleska University, Rosebud, South Dakota.
10. Madeline White, Personal Communication. Sisseton-Dakota.
11. <http://en.wikipedia.org/wiki/Virgo_cluster>.
12. <http://en.wikipedia.org/wiki/Kepler_(spacecraft)>.
13. Seeds, M. 2008. *Stars and Galaxies.* Belmont, CA: Brooks/Cole.
14. <http://en.wikipedia.org/wiki/Milky_Way_Galaxy>.
15. Krupp, E. 1992. *Beyond the Blue Horizon: Myths and Legends of the Sun, Moon, Stars, and Planets.* New York: Oxford University Press.
16. Maryboy, N. and Begay, D. 2010. *Sharing the Skies, Navajo Astronomy.* Tucson: Rio Nuevo Publishers.
17. Sagan, C. 1980. *Cosmos.* New York: Random House.
18. Seeds, M. 2008. *Stars and Galaxies.* Belmont, CA: Brooks/Cole.
19. <http://en.wikipedia.org/wiki/Betelgeuse>.
20. Head, J., L. S. Crumpler, J. Aubele, J. Guest, and R. Saunders. 1992. "Venus Volcansim: Classification of Volcanic Features and Structures, Associations, and Global Distribution from Magellan Data." *Journal of Geophysical Research: Planets* (1991-2012) 97, no. E8: 13153-13197.
21. "Caught in the Wind from the Sun." ESA (Venus Express). 28 November 2007. Retrieved 2008-07-12.

22. Arvol Lookinghorse, Personal Communication.

23. Arvol Lookinghorse, Personal Communication.

24. Buechel, E. and Manhart, P. 2002. *Lakota Dictionary.* Lincoln: University of Nebraska Press.

25. <http://wiki.answers.com/Q/The_original_meaning_of_the_word_month>.

26. Semken, S. 2005. "Sense of Place and Place-Based Introductory Geoscience Teaching for American Indian and Alaskan Native Undergraduates." *Journal of Geoscience Education* 53, 149-157.

27. Cleary, L. Miller and Peacock, T. 1997. *Collected Wisdom: American Indian Education.* Boston: Allyn and Bacon.

28. University of Minnesota, Department of American Indian Studies, <https://filemaker.cla.umn.edu/dakota/recordlist. php>.

CPSIA information can be obtained
at www.ICGtesting.com
Printed in the USA
LVHW072100231220
675004LV00001B/13